Poetic Conduct

Candace J. Durden

Poetic Conduct
Candace J. Durden
_____o_____

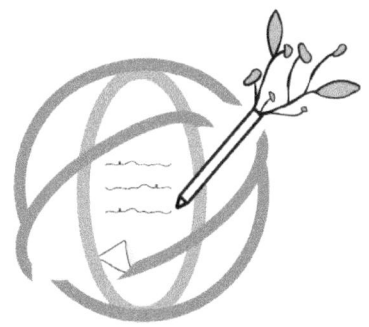

C.J. Durden Press
Altamonte Springs

Writing poetry and short stories, and keeping journals since her teenage years, Candace J. Durden shares her poetry collections with the world. In her style of poetry, Candace offers insight into infatuation, love, and intimacy. Fantasy, friendship, family, and heritage are also explored in this compilation.

Dedication I.

Mom,
Keep me under your wings and protect me with your prayers.

Candace J. Durden
_____o_____

Dedication II.

Candace is the daughter of Kim, the daughter of Mary, Sarah, and Ella, who is the daughter of Amy.

My mother's ancestors carried me, and their spirits are within me.

Candace J. Durden

_____o_____

Acknowledgements

All the glory, honor, and praise are due to God. I've written poetry for years, and I'm delighted to share a collection of poems for the world to read.

A Special Thanks to my husband, Terric. I love you.

I would like to thank my supporters. I appreciate all your contributions to making this publication a success.

The time is now to embark on a journey of *Poetic Conduct* with Candace J. Durden.

Contents

I.
Infatuation

Your Eyes

When you look at me
I feel my heart beat heavily
My stomach full of butterflies
My hands shake
My legs crossed
that's when you look at me
I feel your eyes
connect with mine
It feels good inside

Fantasy

You were a dream about to come true
until I realized
you were only a fantasy turned into an unwanted reality

I thought you were the man I had waited for all my life
You seemed perfect
I expected too much
Became disappointed beyond measure
Convinced that you were the love of my life
My imagination created you
to be the perception of someone else
eager to know you
couldn't get enough of you
you were a mystery
like medicine in my body

Given just enough to function
Anticipated a refill
Hooked until I heard your voice again
The thought of you made my day
Jolly for no apparent reason
Happiness followed
The smile on my face lingered all-day

I thought I was in love
only to discover it was an infatuation
As time progressed, the excitement faded
Recovered from the dose of fantasy
Relieved of your charm
Completely over you
my infatuation
You, my fantasy
My imagination

Pursuit

She first admired him
Soon after, he liked her back
Of course, she was happy, but
something was wrong
He had a girlfriend
He was hesitant
She talked with him
She even brought him roses, candy and
gifted him a picture of herself
on Valentine's Day
Courageous, bold, and forward
and later, he broke up with
his girlfriend
to be with her

Secret Admirers

He looks at me
so, he notices
He spoke to me
so, he's approachable
He stares when he thinks I don't see it
so, he likes me
Does he know that maybe I like him too?
He might or may not even have a clue
I would like to inquire, but when
would I gather the courage?
When will he?
It appears, though,
admirers we will be

Eye Contact

My eyes are saying
I admire you
I adore you
I like you
I want you
My eyes are saying
I like staring at you
I like what I see
I like what I'm doing and
that's making eye contact with you

The Crush

I was really diggin' him and
he didn't even know
It's ironic because, at the same time,
I didn't want it to show
Too shy to speak up and say something
So, I admired him from a distance
I wanted him to have a clue, but
then again, I still didn't want to,
to express interest in a crush
Afraid of rejection and the loss of
a connection
When I see my crush
I blush and seem like I'm doing something in a rush
Even though I know
I try to overlook him
I want to get to know him
I'm just too scared to let the feelings show and
too bashful to tell him and go
Have you ever approached someone and asked,
"Hey, do you like me?"
Didn't think so

I Like You

I hope you ask me out
I'm interested in knowing you
We would make a cute pair
I think so, don't you?
I wish we could hold hands and walk together
You will be my man, I will be your girl
Could this dream come true?
Because boy,
You got me so into you

You Still Do

You still like me
I can see it in your eyes
It's in your stare
How I'm always on your mind
Nervous when you walk by
As I pass you, you watch until
I'm literally out of your sight
Yeah, I know you catch the butterflies
The same way I do
You don't have to give clues
We both know
You like me and
I like you too

Eager

When I think of you,
I have an everlasting smile
A mood that does not escape
It makes me eager to know you more
You say the right things
that spark my interest
I want to know the person you are and
To accept the person you will become
Your faults, your regrets
I hope we will someday feel safe
in each other arms

II.
My King

Black Men

Black men are worthy
with incredible life stories
Black men are earthly Kings
elevated in designated thrones
Your value is greatly known
all around the globe
Industrious in every trade
Innovative in so many ways

Your lineage dynasty is original royalty
with infinite identity
authentic masculinity
athletic physique

Black men are brilliant, intelligent, and magnificent
Black men are needed
The universe cannot exist without you
Black men are husbands, fathers, brothers, nephews, uncles,
sons and cousins
true friends and lovers
Black men are sexy in every way
There's nothing compared to you
when the world sees you in a suit
It's something special about you

Black men are powerful, assertive, and resourceful
your mind, your eyes, your walk, and even in the way you talk
Your smile transfers majestic strength
The touch of you provides kinetic intense

Your kisses taste like joy
Your hugs we all adore
Warm gestures of tender care
You are candid and kind
You are gentle and fine
the way you are
Your presence brings comfort

Black men, you are strong
Black men, you are cherished and
Black men, you are loved
by your precious queens and fellow kings

My Type

I have matured and
blossomed into a woman
I take care of myself
My responsibilities and
Handle my business
That's right

There's somethin' missin'
A man
A strong black man
A no-nonsense type of man
A consistent man
A persistent man
A man with ambition type of man
That's right

He's simple and laid back
Not afraid to be himself type of man
Kind and caring
Intellectual
That's right

He gives affection without having to ask
He opens doors
He's patient and
Waits until I'm ready
That's right

He greets me with a kiss
He cuddles with me before and after
He makes love
He gives good lovin'
It's a joy to be in his presence
My type of man
That's right

My Man

He is good-looking and caring
with his brown caramel, close to almond
complexion
He is beautiful
Handsome
Magnificent
A provider
He is amazing
He's everything that I ever wanted
So true to himself
He is not afraid to be himself
His appearance is admired
Clean low cut and fresh
Goatee to match
He smells good and
He's spontaneous and playful too
My man

HIM

I haven't told him but
he knows
I'm feeling him
I know he wants to be the one
The one for me
It makes him wanna make reservations
to visit, view the scenery and tour the city
He's really diggin' my style
So let's ride

Mine

I wanna make you mine
I want you to be the one
Close by my side
It's just something about you
I like
Don't ask
'Cause I don't know
The way you sometimes
stare into my eyes
It makes me feel something deep inside

III.
Romance Me

Satisfy

You add to my life and make things better
Showing meaning, love, substance, and excitement
Taken me places I've never been and expanded my horizons

Like, you satisfy my appetite
You are the icing on my cake
The butter on my bread and
The honey in my tea

You add to my life and make things better
Showing meaning, love, substance, and excitement
Taken me places I've never been and expanded my horizons

Like, you tap into my soul
You are the dance in my step
The smile of my glow
The stride in my walk
You are the tone of my strength and
The balance of my life

You add to my life and make things better
Showing meaning, love, substance, and excitement
Taken me places I've never been and expanded my horizons

Like, gliding my body
Because you are the music to my ear
The love in my heart
You are the glance in my eyes and
The one on my mind

You add to my life and make things better
Showing meaning, love, substance, and excitement
Taken me places I've never been and expanded my horizons

Addicted

I'm addicted to you
Because I,
I crave you in my thoughts
And desire you in my dreams
I'm hooked on you in my reality
I love the way you
Caress me
Hold me and stroke me
Mentally
Until I'm literally
Captivated by
The sensations you send through my spine

You take me into your arms
And wrap your hands
Around my waist
So firm
So gentle
And I don't want you to let go
No!
You spark so many chills
Instantly,
Constantly,
I'm emotionally
Mesmerized by your touch
Reminded of your sense
Pleased by your kiss
As I stare into your smile

I'm addicted to that
Erotic lust of
Passion

You give to me
You need me
I need you
I want you
Again
And Again,
Once more
I need you
I want you
I'm so glad to have you

Affection

Wrap your tender hands around my waist
It won't hurt to kiss my face
After you held my hands and held them tight
Look me straight into my eyes
Hug me and encourage me
I'll do the same for you
Be sweet to me and
I'll be sweet to you
Show me some affection
Never though temptation
I wouldn't appreciate a confession
For not showing any simple
Affection

IV.
Conduct

Paid In Full

Navient, it was you or the rent
Department of Education was a whole mission
Sallie Mae, goodbye
Annoyed by debt collectors
In this time and era

Deferred payments and hardship claims
Saved all my change
Maintained on limited funds
Bargains were the norm
Searched deals for meals at the store, restaurant and fast food
coupons

Survived personal expenses
Counted dollars and cents
Grace periods were serious
Interest sky-rocketed
Principal balance increased
Quickly sacrificed between wants for needs

From student to a graduate degree
Needed passive income
Sold items at the flea market
Yard sales at my grandma's house
Dinner sales at my auntie's house
Bake sales as a fundraiser
Many visits to the bank
Exchanged coin roll wrappers
For money paper

Deposits, checks, and cash to pay debt collectors
Nearly over a decade and
Now, it's fully paid

Energy Speaks

Energy speaks what's unspoken loudly
Actions followed by predictions of old and recent memories
Uncovered discoveries
Revealed gracefully

Gestures of kindness and courtesy drifted
Existed a short-lived reality

Presented without an uttered word
Unwelcomed acts of ingenuity
Superseded expectations
Unsurprisingly, all unwillingly
Reserved the right to disconnect civilly
From the presence of pretentious company

The Scorned Widow

The mystery of a married couple
Many years lived separate lives
Revealed on the day the husband
Became memorized

A wonder of unanswered questions
Rather the wife would even be present
There, she sat and stood
Emotionless at her husband's farewell service

In an attempt to offer condolences
A scorned widow's response
Unveiled an abrupt reflection of distance and suspension

A widow's refusal of warmth embrace
Uncovered the mystery of a broken marriage
And a scorned widow

Unite

Let us unite to work together
Day and night to rebuild and strengthen
Our communities with powerful resources
To enable us and to disarm the cycle of violence against us

Let us unite to reinvent opportunities and innovations to eradicate
Impoverishment and poverty in our neighboring environments
Let us unite to assist with quality health promotion for our physical
bodies and our mental minds

Let us unite to restore and maintain our schools, colleges, and univer-
sities to continue
To produce a generation of world-class leaders

Let us unite to dismantle slavery,
Mental imprisonment, debt, physical bondage of jails and prisons
Let us unite to create laws that benefit us

Let us unite to raise our children with confidence and competence
towards
Dedication and perseverance for greatness

Let us unite to improve upon yesterday and prepare for tomorrow
Let us unite to eliminate the injustices that happens every day
Let us unite to obtain profitable investments, gainful employment,
and successful
Entrepreneurship that withstands indefinitely

Let us unite to conquer and change the world
Let us unite to reach the dream we all want to live
Let us unite

Battle

It's a battle for people of color
to have the same opportunities as others
It's a battle to end blatant and subtle inequality and social injustices
within the melanated communities
It's a battle to acquire what is rightfully earned and well deserved
when bombarded, oppressed, and afflicted with
covert, overt, and institutional racism
It's a battle to create, receive and maintain the credit of achievements
among
A collective society
It's a battle

V.
Memories

Sweet 16

You've been waiting and anticipating
The time has finally come
You're now sweet 16

The time has arrived
You're more mature and
all grown up now
You're changing every day
Blossoming in your own way
Hoping for new and better things
Sweet 16

As you notice
Turning sweet 16
You begin to see changes
Many changes
What a beautiful age
What a beautiful number
What a beautiful time
Sweet 16

Distant Friend

A close friend felt so distant
A friend no longer near
Our friendship has come to an end
A friendship for only a season

I Miss You

We were close
We talked
You told me your secrets
I told you mine
Do you remember or did time pass us by?
Now, miles away
We talk
But not like we used to
We still write
But of course
Not like we used to
Since you've been gone

Mama's Restoration

As I prayed for recovery over mama's life
I witnessed the restoration of mama's death
There, she rested and smiled upon me
Free of illness
Free of worry
Free of despair
I, too, became free
She laid in peace
Free
Dignified
Angelic
and
Loved
Overcome by her beauty
A shadow of comfort by my side
Reassurance of love and prayer followed me
She surpassed recovery
She was restored

Then and Now

Grandma, you are
Simply beautiful
Too hip
Forever cool
Overly charming
Still forgetful, mainly special
Always refined
Forever classy
Proudly sassy
Hilarious as ever
Fiercely rockin' high heels
The queen of fashion, and
Detailed decorator
Consistent gardener
Extraordinary cook and a fabulous baker
Grandma, a natural-born class act
Brutally honest, best critic, truth teller
Off-the-top jokester
Suddenly outrageous, always unpredictable and
Full of fun and complete laughter
I love you to the sun, the moon, the stars, around the world, and back again

VI.
Healing

Love Is

Love is a beautiful thing
Love is the kindest gift
Love is a friend of mine
Love is patient
Love stays true
Love is forever
Love is a lifetime
Love is everlasting
Love is for better or worse
Love is to cover, not to expose
Love is to care and not to forget
Love is to treat with kindness and not with disrespect
Love is to agree not to prove wrong
Love is to honor and cherish, forever
Love is a feeling but more of an action
You are not to be forced or force someone to love
You, as a decent individual, choose to love
Love someone
It will be a beautiful thing to do

Lovely Recovery

Livin' life in lovely recovery
Lovely recovery
Lovely recovery

Addiction, nonfiction
Real though
For real though
Takin' a kneel to deal with
Spiritual and mental
Demons and heathens intend to win
Do not bend

Wanna live a life of recovery, not misery
You feel me?
Literally

No longer busted, disgusted or
Unfit for society
Forever a child of
The high mighty

Thinkin' clearly
Not cloudy
Busy, daily
Hungry for recovery, amazingly

Stopped chasin' addiction
Racin' to mission
Replacin' poor decisions
Thrivin' sobriety, longevity

Livin' life more safely
Securely,
Gracefully, abundantly
Morally and normally
Accordingly, purposely

The past was wasted
Had to face it
Pacin' and prayin'
Lord forgive me for sinnin'
Believin' a miracle healin'

Strengthenin' devotions
Managin' emotions
Reasonably vocal
Speech was slurred
Soundin' absurd
No longer down
Need a crown!

Facin' emotions
Dealin' in motions
Leavin' relapse in history
Embracin' a new journey
Reclaimin' the victory

Livin' life in lovely recovery
Lovely recovery
Lovely recovery

My Savior

He is my all
My friend
My strength
I love Him so
He'll never leave me
He'll never fail me
He's right there
His love is continual
He'll never stop loving me
He's perfect in every way
I love Him so
His name is forever worthy

Sweet Dedication

Don't give up
Never give up
Overcome your hurt and pain
For the obstacles that get in your way
Fight until the end
With grace, you will conquer through
I believe in you
I know you will get through
And become an inspiration to others
I know you will

The Loss of You

A part of me felt lifeless
Full of sadness
Lost in darkness
Paired with loneliness
Hindered by emptiness
From the loss of you, Mommy

A part of me felt lifeless
Of a broken heart
A clouded mind
Simply disconnected
From the loss of you, Mommy

A part of me felt lifeless
How must I go on?
To live the rest of my life
Without you
From the loss of you, Mommy

My God

I can feel Him
Not in the physical, but in the spiritual
God lives in my heart, down in my soul
I can't see Him, nor touch Him
But I know He's near
I can't see or touch the wind
But I know it's near

Rainbow

Two love birds paired with a smile
Surprised and awakened
By the sunrise after the rain
Excitement blooms for a new journey
A new season to prepare
To share glorious moments of discovery
Gladness and cheer swiftly faded
Suddenly shifted into panic and fear
Emptiness revealed an un-carried joy
A gift returned void
Terror had shattered a sweet dream
Sorrow arrived and pride departed
From dusk to dawn
Hope is renewed
The storm has passed and
A rainbow appeared